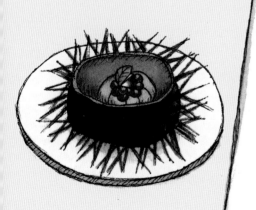

MENU

NIKI NAKAYAMA
A Chef's Tale in 13 Bites

by Jamie Michalak and Debbi Michiko Florence

illustrated by Yuko Jones

Farrar Straus Giroux
New York

For anyone who's ever been told their dream is too big . . .
and dreamed anyway. —J.M.

With love to my husband, Bob, for tremendous support, great
meals, and never giving me cause to say kuyashii. —D.M.F.

To my sons, Hunter and Cameron. May you always
believe in yourselves. Dreams do come true. —Y.J.

Farrar Straus Giroux Books for Young Readers
An imprint of Macmillan Publishing Group, LLC
120 Broadway, New York, NY 10271
mackids.com

In a Los Angeles kitchen, a woman tells a story while cooking. If you were to visit her restaurant, you'd be served thirteen dishes. Each one is a part of her tale. This is the story of that woman, told in thirteen bites.

Come.

Sit.

Taste . . .

Bite 1

Niki Nakayama was born in the United States. Her parents were born in Japan.

Outside of Niki's house was Los Angeles. Inside of her house was Japan.

Sometimes, the two cultures felt very different. But in the kitchen, they became one.

Niki's mother cooked American food with a Japanese twist. Like meatloaf with soy sauce, rice instead of potatoes, and, on Thanksgiving, teriyaki turkey.

Bite 2

One day, Niki's grandmother took her to the market.

"We're going to shop for New Year's dinner," her grandmother said.

"YES!" Niki cheered. "This is the best day of my life!"

Her grandmother laughed. "Doesn't your mother feed you?"

Of course she did. But for Niki, food wasn't just about eating. It was about sharing a table of love and laughter.

"We're going to make a feast," Niki said. "Then we'll all eat together!"

Bite 3

As Niki grew older, she hungered to create her own life story.

She liked to imagine . . . explore . . . and invent!

Most of all, Niki loved making up her own recipes. Like mini pizzas
made from jarred pasta sauce, cheese, and wonton wrappers.

But when she turned twelve, Niki had to help out at the family business—a seafood warehouse for chefs. Niki didn't like the icy building. The fish stared at her with dead eyes.

When I grow up, Niki thought, *I'll do my own thing.*

Bite 4

Niki worked hard at school.

But no matter what she accomplished, her parents had big dreams for one person only— Niki's brother.

"My son will be a success," said Niki's father.

"Always respect your brother," Niki's mother said, "because he's the oldest and a boy."

Niki wished her parents believed she could be a success, too.

She didn't know what she'd be when she grew up, but she knew if she dreamed big and worked hard, she could do anything.

Kuyashii! Niki thought.

"I'll show them!"

Bite 5 After graduating from high school, Niki felt hungry . . . for adventure! She traveled to Tokyo, Japan, where she spent her days discovering the city, one bite at a time. Crunchy fried octopus balls! Slippery udon and ramen noodles! And sweet, chewy mochi!

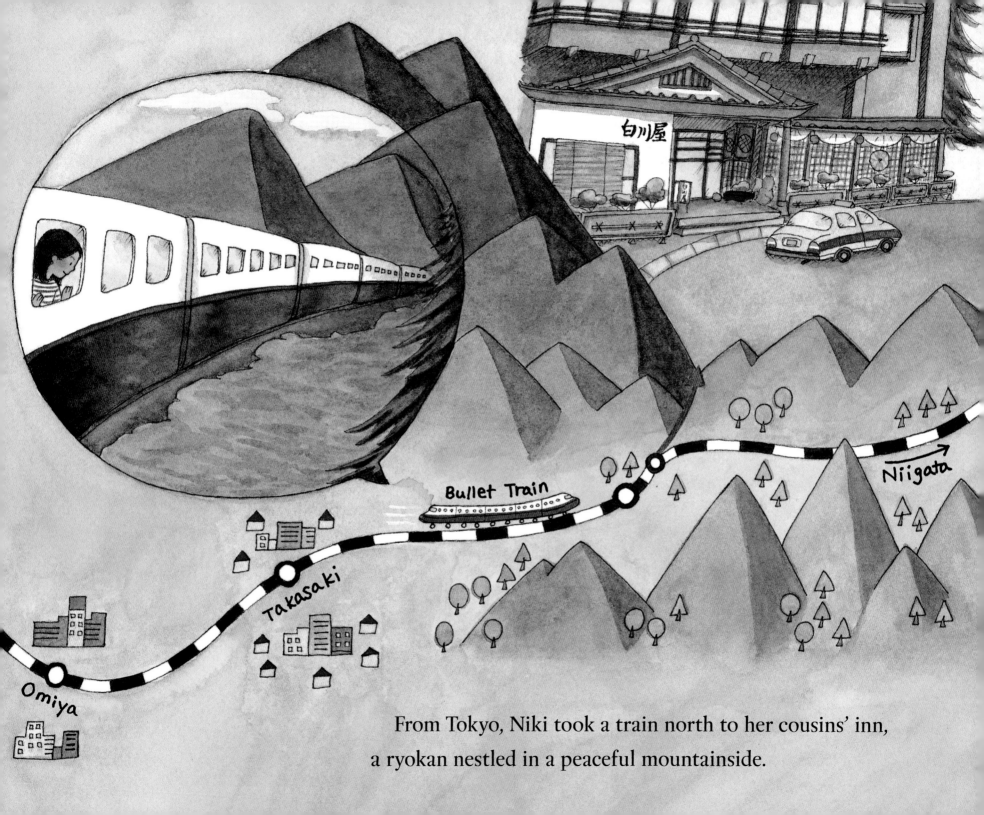

From Tokyo, Niki took a train north to her cousins' inn,
a ryokan nestled in a peaceful mountainside.

Bite 6

There, Niki was served a meal of many courses. One by one, the dishes flowed like a stream.

Each dish was a work of art. Each bite burst with flavor.

The tomato's scent brought back memories of a long-ago picnic.

The corn soup tasted of a warm, lazy day. Together, the courses

told the story of the summer.

Niki learned this storytelling feast had a name: kaiseki.

Inspired, Niki wanted to tell stories with food, too.

Bite 7

When Niki returned home to Los Angeles, she announced,
"I'm going to cooking school!"
"You can't," said her mother. "Chefs are on their feet all day.
Your small body can't handle it."

But Niki went to cooking school anyway. She chopped and measured
and stirred. She began to see food as art—a carrot as a mountain.

Niki's family thought her cooking was just a hobby.

Kuyashii! Niki thought. "I'll show them!"

While in cooking school, Niki got a job at a sushi restaurant.

At first, Chef Izumida wasn't sure Niki could handle working in his kitchen. Female sushi chefs were rare.

"You're just playing chef," he joked.

"This is not play!" Niki said.

She worked harder than anyone. Chef Izumida appreciated her determination.

"Watch and learn," he said. "That's the best way to become a chef."

Niki watched. Niki learned.

Next, she wanted to study kaiseki. Niki followed her heart back to Japan, back to her cousins' inn.

Bite 9

But as far as she knew, female kaiseki chefs didn't exist. In Japan, recipes and cooking techniques were handed down from fathers to sons, male mentors to male apprentices.

"You can't," people told her.

I can, Niki thought.

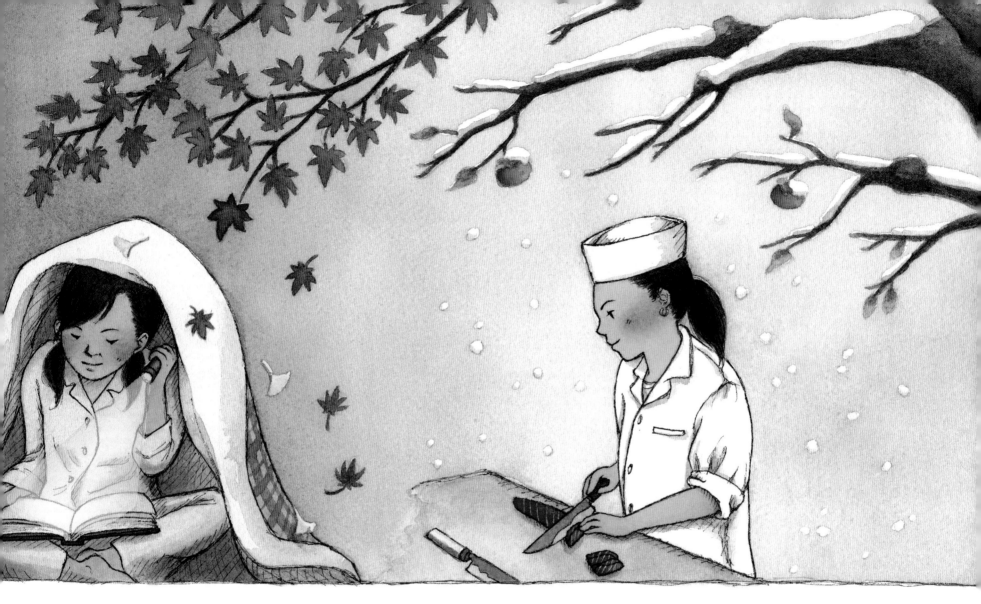

 She tended the garden. She saw snow for the first time. And she discovered
how to tell nature's stories through her cooking.

For three years, Niki watched. Niki learned.

Once again, Niki returned to Los Angeles, but this time with a dream and a plan. "I'm going to open a restaurant," she announced.

"You can't," her family said. "You're not ready."

But Niki convinced them to give her a loan.

Her family agreed, but with one condition: If the restaurant failed, she would have to close it and say goodbye to her dream forever.

Kuyashii! she thought. "I'll show them!"

Niki dreamed of creating kaiseki dishes all her own.

But her mother suggested, "Serve a more familiar food. Sushi."

Niki's heart said no. But she replied, "Yes." She wanted to prove to her family that she could be a success.

From morning till night, she planned and ordered, sliced
and chopped, prepared and plated. She even washed dishes.
By the end of the year, customers lined up at the door.
Finally, Niki knew her parents were proud of her.

But Niki grew tired of making sushi
night after night.

This is not my dream, she thought.

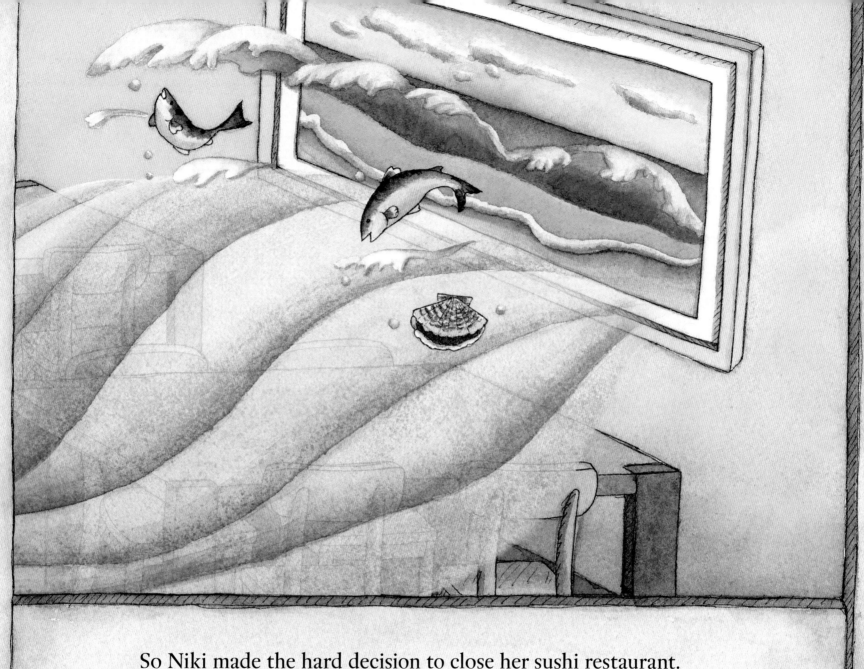

So Niki made the hard decision to close her sushi restaurant.

She worried about what she'd do next.

Then slowly, she began to imagine . . .

. . . and explore . . .

and invent!

The life story she hoped to tell sparkled like the reflection of
sunlight on water. Niki knew exactly what she wanted to do!
It would be difficult. Maybe impossible.

But the voice in her heart said, "Show them."

Niki would serve kaiseki, but she'd do it *her* way. She'd make it Japanese and Californian—just like her. At last, Niki's food would shout, "This is who I am!"

Bite 13

Niki called her new restaurant n/naka. Naka means "inside" in Japanese. Finally, Niki was inside her dream.
She served thirteen courses, making sure they flowed together like a stream.
She cooked with the seasons. Summer meant sweet sorbet using carrots from her garden and bright yellow corn soup.

Niki's dishes were art and story—*her story.*
Word spread about Niki's storytelling food . . .

. . . and customers flowed to n/naka.

Every night, Chef Niki invents delicious dishes. She never serves the same meal to a customer twice.

Every night is like a New Year's celebration of love and laughter.

And whenever anyone says a woman can't be a master chef, Niki lets her food do the talking.

"I'll show them," Niki had said.

And she did.

Ingredients

1974 Niki Nakayama is born in Koreatown, Los Angeles, California. [RICE]

1976 Niki's first memory is of trying her grandmother's okayu, rice porridge, at age two. Her passion for food is born. As she grows older, she enjoys helping her grandmother cook holiday feasts. [PICKLED DAIKON]

1986 At age twelve, Niki begins to work in her family's seafood warehouse, filling out orders for the chefs.
[WONTON PIZZA & RICE CRACKERS]

1995 Niki travels to Tokyo and discovers a variety of flavors that expand her view of what a person can do with food. Next, she travels to Tokamachi to her cousins' ryokan, a Japanese inn, and experiences kaiseki for the first time. [OCTOPUS & CRAB]

1995 Niki attends the Southern California School of Culinary Arts in Pasadena. [CARROT]

1995 Niki interns at the renowned Takao sushi restaurant, where she is mentored by Chef Izumida. [UNI]

1997 Niki returns to her cousins' ryokan in Japan to study kaiseki for three years under Chef Masa Sato. [JAPANESE EGGPLANT]

2000 Niki returns to L.A. and opens Azami Sushi Cafe. When some male customers see a woman behind the sushi counter, they walk out. Her restaurant becomes well-known not only for its food but for having female sushi chefs. [FISH]

2008 Niki closes Azami Sushi Cafe. [SUSHI]

2008 With her sister, Niki opens Inaka. By day, it's a Japanese deli. At night, Niki creates ever-changing, eight-course dinners.

2011 Niki opens n/naka to become perhaps the world's only female kaiseki chef. She keeps notes on every diner so no one ever has the same meal twice. Her signature dish featuring pasta is called Not Bound by Tradition. [PASTA]

2014, 2017–2020 Niki is named a semifinalist for the James Beard Foundation's Best Chefs in America Award. [MOCHI]

2015 Niki marries Chef Carole Iida-Nakayama, who cooks alongside her.

2015 Niki is featured in Netflix's *Chef's Table,* which spotlights international master chefs.

2019 n/naka is awarded two Michelin stars for excellent food.

Kuyashii

In Japanese, there's a word for the defeated feeling that happens when people put you down or say you can't do something: kuyashii.

For Chef Niki, this feeling created a powerful desire to prove her doubters wrong. Over and over, Chef Niki had to protect her dream from those who underestimated her because she is female.

When a famous chef dined at n/naka, he was so impressed with the food that he asked to meet the chef. But when he discovered the chef was a woman, he responded, "Oh, that's cute! So that's how girls cook. How adorable."

His words angered Chef Niki: "There's nothing worse than when people call female chefs and their work cute. It's infuriating."

"When people tell you that you can't do something," she advises, "push even harder. When people say you can't, say, 'Yes I can!'"

By believing in herself and carving her own path, Chef Niki is inspiring a new generation of female itamae, or Japanese chefs. She serves as an example to never let anything stop you from chasing your dreams.

Kaiseki

Kaiseki was first served in sixteenth-century Japan at monastery tea ceremonies. It began as a simple vegetarian meal. Over the centuries, it evolved into a feast of many courses, presented in a certain order for a variety of tastes and textures.

Traditionally served at a ryokan, kaiseki is a meal at one with nature. Kaiseki chefs use what's offered locally each season, like the garden's vegetables, fresh-caught fish, and edible flowers. Each dish reminds diners to enjoy their present time and place.

Chef Niki will never forget the first time she experienced such a meal. After exploring the tastes of Tokyo, she traveled north to her cousin's ryokan in Niigata Prefecture and discovered kaiseki. The map art in this book was drawn at varying scales to reflect her meandering travels and passion for food as she came to understand Japanese cuisine.

Now Chef Niki makes what she calls "modern kaiseki," taking the traditional Japanese culinary art form and interpreting it in her own way. She says, "The best compliment is when guests come and say, 'I can see that it's different from Japanese food, but at the core, it tastes like a Japanese person made it.'" Chef Niki loves that kaiseki is about more than just feeding people. At n/naka, she thanks each of her guests personally. "Kaiseki is about bringing people together," she says, "and making people happy through food."